Plant Life Cycles

HOUGHTON MIFFLIN   BOSTON

Number of Words: 670

Printed in China

ISBN-13: 978-0-618-77032-8
ISBN-10: 0-618-77032-1

2 3 4 5 6 7 8 9-NPC-12 11 10 09 08 07

Contents

How Do Plants Change During Their Life Cycles?

A plant has many parts.
Some parts help plants make new plants.
Some plants have flowers.
Flowers have fruit and seeds.
A **fruit** is the part around a seed.
A **seed** is where a new plant grows.

flower

Almond Tree

Some trees have flowers.
The flowers have seeds inside.
You can plant the seeds.
They will grow into new plants!

fruit

seed

Plant Life Cycles

Living things grow and change.
Living things die, too.
Many changes happen as a living
thing grows.
All of these changes are its
life cycle.

A pea is a seed. It grows
into a pea plant.

Plants have different life cycles.
Most plants start from a seed.
The seed needs warm air and water.
Then it grows into a plant.

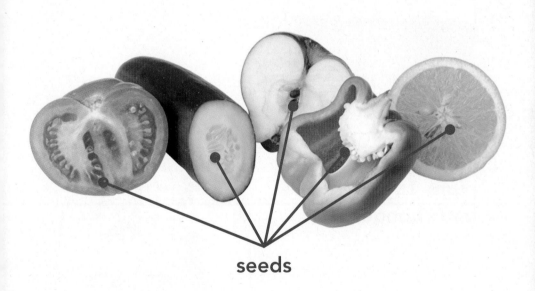

seeds

The plant grows and changes.
It grows leaves and flowers.

The seeds
fall into soil.

The seed grows
into a young
plant. It grows
and changes.

The plant
makes flowers.

The plant dies. The seeds may grow into new plants.

Flowers make fruit. Seeds grow in the fruit.

The flowers make new seeds.
The seeds can grow into new plants.
The life cycle starts again.

Life Cycle of a Pine Tree

Some plants do not have flowers
and fruit.
They have cones.

The seeds fall
into soil.

The seed grows
into a young
tree. It grows
and changes.

A **cone** is like a fruit.
It has seeds.
The cone keeps the seeds safe.

The tree makes cones.

Seeds grow in the cones.

The seeds may grow into new trees.

Sequence

How does a pine tree change as it grows?

2 What Kind of a Plant Grows from a Seed?

A parent plant makes seeds.
The seeds grow into new plants.
The new plants look like the
parent plant.

**This new plant will look
like its parent.**

A trait is the way something looks.
Color, shape, and size are traits.
All living things get traits from
their parents.
They inherit the traits.
Inherit means to have something
passed on.

**Living things inherit traits
from their parents.**

These flowers inherited the same traits.
They have the same leaf shape.
They have the same flower color.
They will grow to be the same size.

Oak Trees and Acorns

Oak trees grow fruit called acorns.
The acorns have seeds.
Acorns fall to the ground.
They can grow into new plants.

acorns

The new plants look like the parent plant.
New plants look like each other, too.
They are all oak trees.
They have flat leaves.
The new plants will grow acorns, too.

oak tree

Draw Conclusions

What kinds of plants always grow from acorns?

3

How Do Plants of the Same Kind Differ?

New plants may look the same. They may look a little different because they can inherit different traits. They may be different sizes. They may be different colors.

These berries inherit color from the parent plant.

New plants may look a little different because of their environment, too. An **environment** is everything around a living thing.
There are living things in an environment.
There are nonliving things, too.

This plant got the right amount of sunlight.

This plant did not.

Differences in a Bigger Group

A **population** is a group of the same kind of living thing in one place.

Look at a population.

You can see ways plants are different.

a population of petunias

These flowers are daffodils.
All the daffodils in a garden are
a population.
The daffodils may not look
the same.
They may be different colors.
They may be different sizes.
But they are all daffodils.

a population of daffodils

Compare and Contrast

How might plants of a population
be the same and different?

How Do Plants React to Their Environment?

4

Gravity pulls all things toward each other.
Gravity changes plants.
It makes the roots of a plant grow down.

Gravity makes roots grow down.

Some plants are changed by touch, too.
If you touch this plant, it will close its leaves.
This keeps the plant safe.

Touch makes this plant close its leaves.

Plants need sunlight.
Some plants grow toward the light.
They bend toward the Sun.
You can turn your plants each day.
This helps them grow straight.

Some plants grow toward light.

Weather Affects Plants

Weather can change how plants grow.
Wind can make plants fall over.
It can even change the shape of a tree.

This tree was bent by wind.

Plants need warm weather.
They can die if it is too hot or cold.
Plants need water, too.
They can die if they have too much
or too little water.

It is too cold for this plant.

Cause and Effect

How can weather change how
plants grow?

Glossary

cone The part of a plant where seeds form in plants without flowers.

cono Parte de la planta donde se forman las semillas de plantas sin flores.

environment All the living and nonliving things around a living thing.

medio ambiente Todos los seres vivos y las cosas sin vida que rodean a un ser vivo.

flower The part of a plant where fruit and seeds form.

flor Parte de la planta donde se forma la fruta y las semillas.

fruit The part of a flower that is around a seed.

fruta Parte de la flor que está alrededorde la semilla.

gravity A force that pulls all objects toward each other.

gravedad Fuerza que empuja entre sí a todos los objetos.

Glossary

inherit To have traits passed on from the parent.

heredar Tener rasgos que provienen del progenitor.

life cycle The series of changes that a living thing goes through as it grows.

ciclo de vida Serie de cambios por los que pasa un ser vivo al crecer.

population A group of the same kind of living thing in one place.

población Grupo del mismo tipo de seres vivos que habitan un lugar.

seed The part of a plant from which a new plant grows.

semilla En una planta, parte de la cual nace una nueva planta.

seed

Think About What You Have Read

❶ A plant part where fruit and seeds form is a _____.

A) flower

B) stem

C) leaf

❷ What stage comes after the seed in a plant's life cycle?

❸ How is a new plant like its parent plant?

❹ Describe the stages of a plant's life cycle.